Bl
10/6

STUDIES IN ENGLISH LITERATURE No. 33

General Editor

David Daiches

Dean of the School of English and American Studies,
University of Sussex

GEORGE GISSING:
NEW GRUB STREET

by
P. J. KEATING

EDWARD ARNOLD (PUBLISHERS) LTD
41 Maddox Street, London W.1

First published 1968

Boards edition SBN: 7131 5375 X
Paper edition SBN: 7131 5376 8

*Printed in Great Britain by
The Camelot Press Ltd., London and Southampton*

General Preface

It has become increasingly clear in recent years that what both the advanced sixth-former and the university student need most by way of help in their literary studies are close critical analyses and evaluations of individual works. Generalisations about periods or authors, general chat about the Augustan Age or the Romantic Movement, have their uses; but all too often they provide merely the illusion of knowledge and understanding of literature. All too often students come up to the university under the impression that what is required of them in their English Literature courses is the referring of particular works to the appropriate generalisations about the writer or his period. Without taking up the anti-historical position of some of the American 'New Critics', we can nevertheless recognise the need for critical studies that concentrate on the work of literary art rather than on its historical background or cultural environment.

The present series is therefore designed to provide studies of individual plays, novels and groups of poems and essays, which are known to be widely studied in sixth forms and in universities. The emphasis is on clarification and evaluation; biographical and historical facts, while they may of course be referred to as helpful to an understanding of particular elements in a writer's work, will be subordinated to critical discussion. What kind of work is this? What exactly goes on here? How good is this work, and why? These are the questions which each writer will try to answer.

DAVID DAICHES

Contents

Contents

Introduction

I

New Grub Street was first published in 1891. It was Gissing's ninth of twenty-two novels, and is easily his most important and enduring work. It holds, however, an unenviable position in the history of the English novel. For although some critics, most notably Q. D. Leavis and Irving Howe, have had no hesitation in proclaiming it a work of art, its continuing interest for the twentieth-century reader lies in Gissing's astute and probing analysis of the 'business of literature'. First and foremost it is a sociological document; a sociological document of genius written in the form of a novel. Awareness of this point has led Irving Howe to conclude that: 'The book is not at all difficult, it is transparent, and to subject it to a "close reading" in the current academic fashion would be tiresome. What *New Grub Street* asks from the reader is not some feat of analysis, but a considered fullness of response, a readiness to assent to, even if not agree with, its vision of defeat.' It is true that an examination of *New Grub Street* for recurrent images and symbolic patterns would not enhance the reader's understanding in the same way as it would with a novel by, say, Dickens, Hardy or Eliot; and it is also true that Gissing's vision is one of defeat. But the 'considered fullness of response' which is demanded from the reader can only be achieved by a complete awareness of the complexity of the issues being analysed, together with an appreciation of the way in which the author presents his case. Neither the argument nor the presentation of the argument is transparent.

Virginia Woolf pointed out that 'Gissing is one of the extremely rare novelists who believes in the power of mind, who makes his people think', and in *New Grub Street* this quality is of particular importance. Not merely does each character represent certain cultural, social or economic forces, but he is continually made to argue the rights and wrongs of his position. It is as a great debate that *New Grub Street* should be viewed; a debate in which certain key words such as 'success', 'failure', 'popular', 'genius', 'conscientious', 'intellectual', and most of all 'practical', recur, developing various shades of irony and ambiguous levels of meaning in such a way that virtually no statement in the book can be taken at face value. Its true meaning will depend on who is speaking, who is being addressed and what stage the debate has reached at that particular moment. The principal speakers fall into three distinct groups; the tradesmen (Milvain and Whelpdale), the artists (Reardon and Biffen) and the men of letters, represented by Alfred Yule. The theme of the debate is the role of literary culture in society, and the central conflict is clearly stated by Milvain in the first chapter:

> 'But just understand the difference between a man like Reardon and a man like me. He is the old type of unpractical artist; I am the literary man of 1882. He won't make concessions, or rather, he can't make them; he can't supply the market. I—well, you may say that at present I do nothing; but that's a great mistake, I am learning my business. Literature nowadays is a trade.'[1]

This, however, is not really the definitive statement it sounds. The basic positions have been established; but the moral, social and cultural issues raised by such an attitude, become clear only when Milvain's bland assumptions are challenged. Is the artist necessarily 'unpractical', and what exactly is meant by the word? Is Milvain stating facts, as he appears to be, or is he merely expressing opinions? Is it reasonable to take Reardon as the archetypal artist or would Biffen be a better example? When Milvain talks of supplying the market, does he mean he is satisfying a demand or creating one? These are just a few of the many questions posed by Gissing and to understand the conflicting answers that are given, and the moral crisis that gradually emerges, the allegorical significance of the major characters must be fully explored.

In terms of form there is little in *New Grub Street* to excite attention. Gissing adopted completely the traditional, though by this time fast disappearing, structure of the three-volume novel. The careers of Milvain and Reardon are shadowed by those of Whelpdale and Biffen, who in their minor roles serve both to adumbrate the major issues and to expand the application of those issues to society as a whole. The

[1] All quotations are taken from *New Grub Street*, 'The World's Classics', London, O.U.P. (1958).

section dealing with the Yule family is employed as a conventional, though thematically relevant, sub-plot; while control of the action lies firmly in the hands of the omniscient author, who has no hesitation in addressing the reader in order to point the moral or underline a note of irony.

Yet in spite of the use of this unwieldy novel form ('a triple-headed monster, sucking the blood of English novelists', as Milvain describes it), *New Grub Street* attains a remarkable degree of unity. This is achieved by a concentration on the careers of a handful of characters, who in their relationships with each other provide a microcosmic view of society. Gissing's method relies heavily on a massive accumulation of detail (intellectual, social, and conversational) which, carefully organised and placed, is used to build up a complex ironic structure. By this means he creates an illusion of having presented to the reader a complete cross-section of the literary life of London. Yet the vicious Fadge, Markland the popular novelist, Jedwood the new type of publisher, the reviewers, the critics, and the society figures who wield such influence, none of the people who dictate the conditions within which the action takes place, ever actually appear in the novel. They exist in a world beyond Reardon's reach; a world to which Milvain goes and returns to report upon. Only in the final chapter do Milvain's influential friends appear, and then when Reardon is dead and Milvain himself is in a position to be both editor and host. The two worlds are completely incompatible. The success of one entails the annihilation of the other.

Where the two worlds do come together is in their role as guardians of the nation's taste, and they are united in the British Museum Reading-room, which is employed throughout the novel as a symbol of the accumulated knowledge of mankind. Milvain describes Alfred and Marian Yule as 'obvious dwellers in the valley of the shadow of books', and his flowery remark anticipates the moment when Marian, gazing up at the Reading-room dome sees herself and the other researchers as 'hapless flies caught in a huge web, its nucleus the great circle of the Catalogue'. Reardon's response is totally different. He looks back upon his early days in London and remembers the Reading-room as 'his true home', and when the drudgery of his three-volume novel is over he relaxes in the Museum, indulging his love of the classics by writing essays on esoteric literary themes. In Chapter VII the Reading-room is seen as a place of lost causes and sterile academic work. Mr. Hinks presents Marian with a copy of his 'Essay on the Historical Drama' for her father; and Mr. Quarmby passes on his private information that Alfred Yule is at last to be offered the editorship he longs for—the gossip is as worthless as the book. The courtship between Marian and Milvain is conducted largely from the British Museum; he hurriedly consulting encyclopaedias and she dreaming of the day when a machine will be invented to take over her thankless task. Finally the Reading-room is the place where all illusions are shattered. Alfred Yule refuses to discuss his coming blindness with his daughter, dismissing her with: 'You can read up the subject for yourself at the British Museum.' And when Biffen plans to poison himself it is to the Reading-room he goes for the necessary knowledge.

This symbolic use of the British Museum is extremely successful but in the main Gissing did not feel at home with symbolism. Nothing could be more crude, for instance, than the moment in Chapter III when Milvain asks Marian to indulge him in a spot of 'childishness' and go to watch the London express rush under a bridge. This experience is meant to symbolize both his driving ambition and the disconcerting sexual attraction Marian possesses for him; but the symbol is local and is not integrated into the novel. It is unnecessary and thus distracting. On the other hand, symbolic images, such as the hanged man or the worn-out horse, grow and develop as the novel progresses, heightening the moral uncertainty of a rapidly changing society. In this instance, as in all others, Gissing's craftsmanship is uneven, and his weaknesses should be acknowledged. His writing is at times ponderous and artificially literary and suffers from all of the faults he notes in Reardon's work and some of those in Alfred Yule's. Further, he often seriously underestimates the intelligence of the reader (a significant fault in the author of a book such as *New Grub Street*), and insists on too heavily underlining the motives and emotions of the characters. His sense of humour is best described in the same terms that Biffen uses to excuse Reardon's feeble riddle: 'It'll pass. Distinctly professional though. The general public would fail to see the point.'

He was a morbidly autobiographical novelist and this has, perhaps, prevented his best work from receiving the critical attention it deserves. Gissing's greatest admirers have often been so busy sifting the novels for biographical analogies that the work itself has been ignored. This is particularly true of *New Grub Street* and is a tendency which should be resisted. Sometimes, as in the portrait of Reardon, Gissing becomes too personally involved and this is a flaw which needs to be recognised, but, in this novel at least, Gissing usually succeeds in distancing himself from the action, and his own attitudes should be judged only when the total pattern of the work has been considered.

II

In terms of subject matter *New Grub Street* is virtually unique. Novels about novelists there have been in plenty but they tend either to concentrate on aspects of the novelist's life other than his writing; or they deal intimately with the growth of a single mind or sensibility. If one compares, for example, *David Copperfield* (1850) and *Pendennis* (1850) on the one hand, and *Portrait of the Artist as a Young Man* (1916) on the other, the change in treatment is astounding. Neither David Copperfield nor Arthur Pendennis seem to feel that being a writer is anything to make much of a fuss about.[1] It is a profession which can bring both financial rewards and a place in society. It demands talent and a degree of worldly experience, but not creative agony. Such an attitude is meaningless to Stephen Dedalus. Society is something to escape from, and the very thought that one's work might bring public acclamation is enough to brand one as an inferior artist. The period of Gissing's life (1857–1903) coincides almost exactly with the most important phase of this complex revolution, and historically it is significant that the work nearest in tone to *New Grub Street* is the group of short stories on literary themes written by Henry James in the early 1890s.

[1] *Pendennis* does, however, contain some superb ironic chapters on the world of journalism. It was a novel much admired by Gissing and could well have been an influence on *New Grub Street*. Compare, for instance, Milvain's view of 'genius' with that of Warrington (*Pendennis*, Chapter XXXII).

The relevance of the title *New Grub Street* is primarily historical. There are several exact comparisons (principally with reference to the work of Reardon and Alfred Yule) but Gissing usually employs the phrase *Grub Street* in either a vaguely emotional or pejorative sense, or to establish an historical frame of reference. That he was fully aware of the various shades of meaning that surround the phrase is made clear in a letter he wrote to his German friend Eduard Bertz on the 26th April, 1891. He writes: 'Grub Street actually existed in London some hundred and fifty years ago. In Pope and his contemporaries the name has become synonymous for wretched-authordom. In Hogarth's "Distressed Author" there is "Grub Street" somewhere inscribed. Poverty and meanness of spirit being naturally associated, the street came to denote an abode, not merely of poor, but of in-insignificant, writers.' He goes on to quote Dr. Johnson's famous definition: 'Originally the name of a street near Moorfields in London, much inhabited by writers of small histories, dictionaries, and temporary poems; whence any mean production is called *grubstreet*.' Later in the same letter Gissing says: 'At present the word is used contemptuously. You know that I do not altogether mean that in the title of my book.'

On one level Gissing is indicating that late Victorian England has created a Grub Street as pernicious as that which existed in the early eighteenth century. Many of the central issues such as the power of the publishers, the suffering and poverty of the authors, the hack-writing of the journalists, the virtual impossibility for anyone—save a genius —to rise out of Grub Street once he is there, the superabundance of mediocre work being churned out for an audience forever demanding more of the same—all this and more is relevant to both periods. But on another level Gissing is implying that *New* Grub Street is in many ways a logical development of the old. They are not two isolated periods, but both parts of a process of change (what Raymond Williams has called 'The Long Revolution') which will lead ultimately to a culturally fragmentated society. The chief historical fact Gissing has in mind when he refers back to the early eighteenth century is the rise of a large commercial middle class, together with the corresponding development of newspapers, the novel and the periodical. These are, of course, the very literary forms with which

New Grub Street is concerned and each is shown to have suffered, in the process of time, fearful corruption. Jasper Milvain is the modern equivalent of Addison or Steele; Alfred Yule is surely Dr. Johnson; and a popular novelist such as Richardson has become Markland. Characters such as Whelpdale, Fadge and Jedwood are the eternal vampires feeding, consciously or unconsciously, on the blood of struggling writers. This last comparison pinpoints more exactly Gissing's personal attitude to Grub Street, for in some ways he is indulging in a spot of myth-making. It is believed by everyone in *New Grub Street* that genius, true, unadulterated genius, will either rise out of the mire and receive its just acclaim or will suffocate and die scornful of all material reward. Given the social conditions it is more natural that the latter will occur, but genius is *sui generis* and it could just as easily follow the former course. Whatever eventually happens, however, the possessor of genius will, at first, be forced to join the writers in Grub Street. He is not a hack himself but he must rise from the ranks of the hacks, or rather, dwell with them by necessity. Milvain expresses the accepted view: 'I am speaking of men who wish to win reputation before they are toothless. Of course if your work is strong, and you can afford to wait, the probability is that half a dozen people will at last begin to shout that you have been monstrously neglected, as you have.'

A further analogy being made between the two Grub Streets is the use made of literature to advance personal squabbles and vendettas. 'To assail an author without increasing the number of his readers is the perfection of journalistic skill', writes Gissing, and everyone, whether tradesman, artist or man of letters, enjoys a good literary slanging match. When Fadge's periodical, *The Study*, publishes two conflicting reviews of the same novel, Alfred Yule is delighted because he hates Fadge, Milvain and Reardon roar with laughter because the error confirms their totally different views of the market, and even Biffen raises a chuckle.

The main issues examined by Gissing have all become commonplaces of twentieth-century critical thought and discussion. The alienation of the artist from society; the development of a new kind of popular press; an increasingly centralised society dominated by London; the new concept of the art of fiction; and the conscious acceptance by everyone involved of the intellectual, commercial and cultural division of English life. In Chapter XXIX Alfred Yule sums up the situation in a suitably pedantic manner:

> 'How much better "a man of letters" than "a literary man"! And apropos of that, when was the word "literature" first used in our modern sense to signify a body of writing? In Johnson's day it was pretty much the equivalent of our "culture". You remember his saying, "It is surprising how little literature people have." His dictionary, I believe, defines the word as "learning, skill in letters"— nothing else.'

It is the forces making for this change that Gissing sets out to analyse and in doing so brilliantly captures a crucial moment in a period of cultural crisis.

1. *Tradesmen*

New Grub Street opens and closes with Jasper Milvain. In the first chapter the conversation he has with his mother and sisters over the breakfast table serves both to establish the central conflict of the novel, and to indicate the strain of self-deception in his character. The clock striking eight reminds him that there is a man being hanged in London at that moment. At first he adopts a facetious pose saying, 'There's a certain satisfaction in reflecting that it is not oneself.' Rebuked by his sister for selfishness he switches to his characteristic mode of defence which is to evaluate all events in terms of success or failure:

> 'A man who comes to be hanged . . . has the satisfaction of knowing that he has brought society to its last resource. He is a man of such fatal importance that nothing will serve against him but the supreme effort of law. In a way, you know, that is success.'

Jasper is obviously referring to his own ambition to become both the manipulator of cultural forces and an object of social veneration. The cynical turning upside down of normal social values is to be the means by which he is to attain these ends. In the world of New Grub Street, however, the hanged man is the artist who comes to solitary death not by stirring 'society to its last resource', but by being totally ignored. It is not success but failure, and Milvain is not the hanged man but the hang-man.

For Milvain is the chief defendant of a commercially divided culture. His argument is simple. If a market demand exists then it should be satisfied, and 'we people of brains are justified in supplying the mob with the food it likes'. The intellectual is to do the writing because he alone has the ability to develop the necessary talents, which must be flexible enough to fulfil the requirements of different types of demand:

> 'If only I had the skill, I would produce novels out-trashing the trashiest that ever sold fifty thousand copies. But it needs skill, mind you: and to deny it is a gross error of the literary pedants. To please

B

the vulgar you must, one way or another, incarnate the genius of
vulgarity.'

It is Milvain's chief regret that he is incapable of carrying out this
particular scheme, but his sights are set on a group of people just as
vulgar, fewer in number, but with more money:

> 'I shall write for the upper middle-class of intellect, the people who
> like to feel that what they are reading has some special cleverness,
> but who can't distinguish between stones and paste.'

It is not that Milvain himself has anything special to say. His intention
is simply to play up to the intellectual snobbery of his readers; to
develop a style which employs the smart phrase and the glib sentiment
as a substitute for thought. To Old John Yule he openly confesses that
he writes about 'nothing in particular. I make a salable page or two out
of whatever strikes my fancy', and when Dora queries his qualifica-
tions for writing a certain article he answers: 'It is my business to
know something about every subject—or to know where to get the
knowledge.' He completely despises his readers, viewing them as
being incapable of any kind of critical judgement. His advice to Maud
in Chapter XXVIII, is typical of the way his generalisations move
from a specific group of readers to cover the market as a whole:

> 'You must remember that the people who read women's papers are
> irritated, simply irritated, by anything that isn't glaringly obvious.
> They hate an unusual thought. The art of writing for such papers—
> indeed, for the public in general—is to express vulgar thought and
> feeling in a way that flatters the vulgar thinkers and feelers.'

According to Milvain people are vulgar if they cannot see that they
are being got at by the writer. Journalism is essentially ephemeral and
if it is to succeed it must make an immediate, but certainly not a
sensational, impact (sensations are for a class of readers even more
vulgar than Milvain's). Because he is incapable of thinking for himself the reader must be wooed with superficial material dressed up in a
style of writing which can be immediately recognised and praised as
'clever'. Milvain has already carefully studied this particular skill, and
one of his highest literary ambitions is to employ it in writing the

minor leaders for a big daily newspaper: 'The kind of thing in which one makes a column out of what would fill six lines of respectable prose. You call a cigar a "convoluted weed", and so on, you know; that passes for facetiousness. I've never really tried my hand at that style yet; I shouldn't wonder if I managed it brilliantly.'

One of Milvain's favourite words is 'intellect'. He believes himself to be liberally endowed with this quality and the highest praise he can give to anyone he admires is to call him an 'intellectual'. But Milvain is not an intellectual in any sense of the word which Biffen, Reardon or Alfred Yule would recognise. He never joins in the discussions on classical literature or aesthetic theory which enliven the evenings of Biffen and Reardon, but always arrives just too late or swings the conversation around to the exigencies of the commercial market. He quotes the great writers of the past with a show of familiarity but always with such exact relevance to his own position that the original meaning is completely falsified. Thus in Chapter XXII when 'manufacturing copy', and finding great difficulty in doing so, 'Dr. Johnson's saying, that a man may write at any time if he will set himself doggedly to it, was often upon his lips.' At other times he quotes Dumas to support his argument that any kind of publicity is good publicity; Keats to help postpone his marriage to Marian; Landor to justify his own desire for wealth; and Burns to give moral support to his selfseeking.

Furthermore, although he defends his own 'conscientiousness' on intellectual grounds, he does not allow the same kind of praise to others. Even with his friends he is unwilling to acknowledge any kind of 'worth' other than financial. No one is more conscientious than Biffen who is described by Milvain as pegging away at 'an interminable novel, which no one will publish when it's done'; and Whelpdale's experiments in the realistic manner are dismissed with, 'You may write what you like, so long as people are willing to read you.' He even goes so far as to say that Reardon 'is absurd enough to be conscientious'. On the other hand the slashing review by Fadge of Alfred Yule's book is praised by Milvain for having been done 'vilely well'. For Milvain recognises no intermediate stages between work of 'genius' and 'good, coarse, marketable stuff'. His defence of such a view is, as always, deceptively simple: 'Oh, if you can be a

George Eliot, begin at the earliest opportunity. I merely suggested what seemed practicable. But I don't think you have genius, Maud. People have got that ancient prejudice so firmly rooted in their heads —that one mustn't write save at the dictation of the Holy Spirit. I tell you, writing is a business.' If a writer possesses genius, he argues, then no rules apply, but if not 'and we sit down in a spirit of long-eared gravity we shall produce only commonplace stuff'. His self-proclaimed intellectual superiority is based entirely upon his perception of this distinction:

> 'There are few men in London capable of such a feat. Many a fellow could write more in quantity, but they couldn't command my market. It's rubbish, but rubbish of a very special kind, of fine quality.'

But even here Milvain's attitude is not so straightforward as it seems. When Old John Yule attacks 'the business of literature' Milvain springs to the defence claiming that 'it helps to spread civilisation'. Yet to Reardon he confesses, 'Never in my life shall I do anything of solid literary value; I shall always despise the people I write for. But my path will be that of success.' Contradictory attitudes like these reflect the feeling of guilt that lies beneath the apparent self-confidence; a guilt which he tries to assuage by sharing his great discovery with his unpractical friends, and by attempting to use his literary skill and influential patrons to help others up the ladder of success—provided that they mean the same by 'success' as he does. His sisters do follow his advice and make their mark on the literary world, but by the close of the book even they are alienated from him; while the uselessness of his advice to men such as Reardon and Biffen is shown in Chapter XXXIII, one of the key sections of the whole novel.

Reardon's death has occurred in the preceding chapter and Biffen's novel has just appeared. Gissing's own hostility is shown in his reference to 'Jasper of the facile pen', who, in a great burst of virtuosity, produces two reviews of *Mr. Bailey, Grocer;* the one eulogistic, the other slightly more reserved, to be published in different periodicals. Milvain's personal view of the novel—'If I knew a doctor who had many cases of insomnia in hand, I would recommend "Mr.

Bailey" to him as a specific'—has nothing to do with the task in hand. It is a simple act of friendship which must be defended before the very people who are admiring his skilful change of styles:

> 'The struggle for existence among books is nowadays as severe as among men. If a writer has friends connected with the press, it is the plain duty of those friends to do their utmost to help him. What matter if they exaggerate, or even lie? The simple, sober truth has no chance whatever of being listened to, and it's only by volume of shouting that the ear of the public is held.'

He follows this up by reading aloud an article he has written on 'The Novels of Edwin Reardon', which deeply moves his audience. As Gissing ironically points out, 'One who knew Jasper might reasonably have doubted, before reading this, whether he was capable of so worthily appreciating the nobler man.' The belated tribute can do little even for Reardon's reputation: it does, however, convince his surviving friends and relations of Milvain's humanity, and it also brings the practical man back into contact with Amy. It is further significant that Milvain's recital follows immediately upon the discussion inspired by Whelpdale's scheme to provide reading matter for the quarter-educated.

That Milvain's much vaunted intellect is merely a form of conceit is indicated in many ways. He is shown to possess certain qualities as a writer which are by no means neglible. His sense of observation is very highly developed and his understanding of the needs of the commercial market comes from a prolonged study of the habits and behaviour patterns of the different classes. These qualities are particularly useful to the novelist and the fact that it is Milvain, the journalist, who possesses them is intended as an ironic comment on Reardon's continual search for 'inspiration'. Milvain himself cannot write novels because he is deficient in the qualities of love and sympathetic understanding; a personal failing which is most apparent in the love scenes with Marian. His genuine ability to use words, however, is recognised by everyone. What is important to note is the kind of praise given to him. Seen through the eyes of others he is always 'clever', 'smart', 'popular', 'skilful', or 'practical'. These, of course, are the qualities which he himself equates with intellect, but within the framework of the novel they are shown to be corruptive. The people who stand aside from his advice all symbolise the finer values which are slowly being crushed out of society (e.g. Reardon, Biffen, and to a lesser degree Dora). Those who follow his advice prosper but are either morally corrupted or become the agents of moral corruption (e.g. Whelpdale, Maud and Amy).

His courtship of Marian represents what is for him a falling away from his high standards of cynicism: 'It had to be confessed that he was the victim of a vulgar weakness. He had declared himself not of the first order of progressive men,' and her destruction is thus essential if he is to regain his self-respect. When, in Chapter XXX, he at last manages to get her to admit that the luxuries he desires do 'enable one to live a better and fuller life', then, at that moment, she too is corrupted. The love which she had grasped at as a means of escape from literary slavery must be sacrificed to Milvain's social ambitions. It recalls the scene in Chapter VIII when he compulsively confesses to Marian, 'I shall do many a base thing in life, just to get money and reputation; I tell you this that you mayn't be surprised if anything of that kind comes to your ears.' It is a statement which ironically anticipates the basest action he commits.

It is important to note that Milvain is not only an agent of corruption but is himself morally corrupted. To meet and become friendly with—if possible, to become essential to—wealthy and influential people is a cornerstone of his literary theories: 'Men won't succeed in literature that they may get into society, but will get into society that they may succeed in literature.' Just as he equates his own particular type of talent with intellectual power so he declares that 'the end of literary work—unless one is a man of genius—is to secure comfort and repute'. As he begins to make a reputation with his witty and cynical articles he grows increasingly impatient with his lack of social position. It is not merely the need to marry a wealthy woman—this he has avowed from the beginning—but rather a terrifying heightening of his powers of self-deception and a gradual decline of his one saving grace, wit. In the first chapter he is shown to be living at the expense of his mother who can barely afford it. He justifies his meanness on the grounds that he is merely serving his apprenticeship and will later repay everything in full, and when his mother attempts to recover a debt owed to her by relatives even poorer than herself Milvain sincerely opposes such action because, 'One doesn't like to do brutal things if one can avoid them.' This is at the beginning of his career, but by the time of Reardon's death he has fully accepted the fact that the system he advocates can only survive by doing brutal things.

He has quite consciously contributed to the misunderstanding between Reardon and Amy, and openly gauges his love for Marian according to her fluctuating financial fortunes. Even while he is still engaged to her he searches around for someone with even more money to whom he can propose marriage. This moral decline is emphasised by his increasing coarseness of mind and speech. He has built up his reputation by playing with values and words, turning the traditional or the respected meanings on their heads; and now this corrupt strain dominates his actions in a new way. He justifies his proposal to the masculine Miss Rupert on the grounds that she would be a fit 'intellectual' partner for him. He rebukes Marian for being 'matter-of fact', and in Chapter XXXVI, in order to keep his promise to Dora that he will at last ask Marian to marry him immediately, he is forced to juggle with words and feelings so that Marian is placed in such a position that *she* is obliged to refuse him. He speaks sarcastically to his sisters; returns Whelpdale's adulation with sneers, and now thinks so highly of his intellectual superiority that he can abuse Maud's wealthy husband: 'But he must treat *me* with respect. My position in the world is greatly superior to his. And, by the gods! I will be treated respectfully!' His proposal to Miss Rupert rejected, he comes to realise that 'he lived in eager expectation of the word which should make him rich'.

It is important to recognise this strain of coarseness in Milvain's character as otherwise the full meaning of the final scene in the book is obscured. Married to Amy, who has herself undergone a similar process of moral corruption, he has achieved all his ambitions. He is not merely the conqueror of society but society itself:

'Happiness is the nurse of virtue.'
'And independence the root of happiness.'
'True. "The glorious privilege of being independent"—yes, Burns understood the matter. Go to the piano, dear, and play me

something. If I don't mind, I shall fall into Whelpdale's vein, and talk about my "blessedness". Ha! isn't the world a glorious place?'

'For rich people.'

'Yes, for rich people. How I pity the poor devils!—Play anything. Better still if you will sing, my nightingale!'

So Amy first played and then sang, and Jasper lay back in dreamy bliss.

II

Whelpdale, like Milvain, is a 'man of his day' with the significant difference that he has served his apprenticeship in the old school. He represents the failed artist who discovers that he possesses a natural understanding of the requirements of the commercial market and turns dull defeat into brilliant success. In one sense he is a traitor and his ambiguous position is reflected in Gissing's mocking treatment of him and in the mixture of contempt and affection with which the opposing camps regard him.

He is first mentioned in the second chapter when Milvain refers to him in passing as 'that ass Whelpdale'. His name does not appear again until the close of Chapter X when a significant conversation takes place:

'I can't understand how his book should be positively refused,' said Reardon. 'The last wasn't altogether a failure.'

'Very nearly. And this one consists of nothing but a series of conversations between two people. It is really a dialogue, not a novel at all. He read me some twenty pages, and I no longer wondered that he couldn't sell it.'

'Oh, but it has considerable merit,' put in Biffen. 'The talk is remarkably true.'

'But what's the good of talk that leads to nothing?' protested Jasper.

'It's a bit of real life.'

'Yes, but it has no market value. You may write what you like, so long as people are willing to read you. Whelpdale's a clever fellow, but he can't hit a practical line.'

'Like some other people I have heard of,' said Reardon, laughing.

'But the odd thing is, that he always strikes one as practical-minded. Don't you feel that, Mrs. Reardon?'

The fact that it is Biffen who acknowledges the merit of Whelpdale's novel makes it clear that Whelpdale's later change of sides has nothing to do with his inability to produce good (i.e. artistic) work. Like every other character he must make the basic choice between devotion to art or to the market. Biffen, Reardon and Milvain have already reached their decision; Whelpdale is the only waverer and when Milvain praises him for possessing the key virtue, a practical mind, it is a positive indication which side he is eventually to join. Two chapters later there is a further conversation concerning Whelpdale's career when his friends learn, through a newspaper advertisement, that he has set up as a 'literary adviser'. While Reardon is indignant it is Milvain who points the moral: 'Now that's one of the finest jokes I ever heard. A man who can't get anyone to publish his own books makes a living by telling other people how to write!'

When Whelpdale does finally appear, in Chapter XVI, there is no longer any doubt about the role he is to play. This rather farcical scene in which he is jilted by the Birmingham girl with whom he is in love, has sometimes been seen as a kind of comic interlude which is ruined by Gissing's heavy-handedness. But it is really an important detail in the building up of Whelpdale's character. His romantic view of women and his inability to find anyone to return his love, is in marked contrast to the flow of practical ideas which pour out of him once he abandons any pretence of being an artist. His insensitivity, naïvety, and lack of self control is frequently stressed. Biffen and Reardon are horrified when Whelpdale speaks of his fiancée's consumption as though it provided her with an added physical attraction. He eagerly discusses his many frustrated attempts to marry; insincerely praises Reardon's worthless novel, and lavishes an undeserved eulogy on Dora's magazine serial. It is yet another irony in the structure which Gissing is building up, for in *New Grub Street* Whelpdale emerges from the conflict as the most influential literary figure of them all. It is Whelpdale, not Milvain, who revolutionises the mass media and whose influence is thus felt throughout the country. He does not possess the wit or the skill of Milvain, nor the intellect or sensibility of Reardon and Biffen. He is the complete tradesman whose merchandise is ideas, and because he is a traitor his ideas are based upon information gathered from the artistic failure of himself and his friends. He has no appreciation of the true nature of the cultural conflict in which he is playing so large a part and is thus never regarded as being fully responsible for his actions. Every plan he outlines is serving to cut the ground away from under the feet of his artist friends, yet he never understands this. His sole moral guide is that he is supplying an already existing market demand:

'What do you think I'm writing just now? An author's Guide. You know the kind of thing; they sell splendidly. Of course I shall make it a good advertisement of my business. Then I have a splendid idea. I'm going to advertise: "Novel-writing taught in ten lessons!" What do you think of that? No swindle; not a bit of it. I am quite capable of giving the ordinary man or woman ten very useful lessons.'

It is a mark of Whelpdale's complete lack of sympathetic understanding that he outlines the synopsis of his Guide for Reardon's 'amusement':

'I gravely advise people, if they possibly can, to write of the wealthy middle class; that's the popular subject, you know. Lords and ladies are all very well, but the real thing to take is a story about people who have no titles, but live in good Philistine style. I urge study of horsey matters especially; that's very important. You must be well up, too, in military grades, know about Sandhurst, and so on. Boating is an important topic. You see?'

Whelpdale's great scene (Chapter XXXIII) follows immediately upon Reardon's death, and marks the culminating rationalisation of the social forces which had inspired in the one writer a drive to commercial success, and in the other a death wish. Whelpdale's career now takes a spectacular turn. The man who had written short stories in America to save himself from starving, who failed as a realistic novelist, who began to pick up as a literary adviser, who tasted success with his author's Guide, and who took a step forward as compiler of an information column in *Chat-Moss*, now employs his gradually acquired knowledge in an enterprise which involves the whole of English society:

'I want to find a capitalist,' he said, 'who will get possession of that paper *Chat*, and transform it according to an idea I have in my head.

The thing is doing very indifferently, but I am convinced it might be made splendid property, with a few changes in the way of conducting it.'

'The paper is rubbish,' remarked Jasper, 'and the kind of rubbish —oddly enough—which doesn't attract people.'

'Precisely, but the rubbish is capable of being made a very valuable article, if it were only handled properly. I have talked to the people about it again and again, but I can't get them to believe what I say. Now just listen to my notion. In the first place, I should slightly alter the name; only slightly, but that little alteration would in itself have an enormous effect. Instead of *Chat* I should call it *Chit-Chat*.'

Jasper exploded with mirth.

'That's brilliant!' he cried. 'A stroke of genius!'

'Are you serious? Or are you making fun of me? I believe it *is* a stroke of genius. *Chat* doesn't attract anyone, but *Chit-Chat* would sell like hot cakes, as they say in America. I know I am right; laugh as you will.'

This scheme is on a scale which excites even Milvain to admiration, but Whelpdale, lacking the cynicism of his idol, is perfectly serious in seeing himself as a kind of public benefactor:

'I would have the paper address itself to the quarter-educated; that is to say, the great new generation that is being turned out by the Board schools, the young men and women who can just read, but are incapable of sustained attention. People of this kind want something to occupy them in trains and on 'buses and trams. As a rule they care for no newspapers except the Sunday ones; what they want is the lightest and frothiest of chit-chatty information—bits of stories, bits of description, bits of scandal, bits of jokes, bits of statistics, bits of foolery. Am I not right? Everything must be very short, two inches at the utmost; their attention can't sustain itself beyond two inches. Even chat is too solid for them: they want chit-chat.'

When Dora objects that 'these poor, silly people oughn't to be encouraged in their weakness', Jasper is at hand to prop up the dejected Whelpdale. Between them they sketch out the whole shabby justification of such a venture. *Chit-Chat* will be read only on train journeys; it will be informative; it will encourage a taste for serious reading; the leading 'sensational' item such as 'What the Queen Eats', or 'How Gladstone's collars are made', would always be counter-balanced by 'nicely written little accounts of exemplary careers, of heroic deeds and so on'. Gissing leaves no doubt in the reader's mind about where he stands on this issue: 'Whelpdale's noteworthy idea triumphed; the weekly paper called *Chat* was thoroughly transformed, and appeared as *Chit-Chat*. From the first number, the success of the enterprise was beyond doubt; in a month's time all England was ringing with the fame of this noble new development of journalism.' But it is left for Milvain to explain to Dora just what exactly Whelpdale's idea can lead to. Travelling to Sark they see a copy of *Chit-Chat* in the hands of an 'obese and well-dressed man':

'Is *he* one of the quarter-educated?' asked Dora, laughing.
'Not in Whelpdale's sense of the word. But, strictly speaking, no doubt he is. The quarter-educated constitute a very large class indeed; how large, the huge success of that paper is demonstrating.'

The crowning point of Whelpdale's career is his marriage to Dora Milvain, one of the few completely admirable characters in the novel. Only those who succeed deserve a beautiful and intelligent wife, and in the eyes of society what Whelpdale has achieved is deserving of great recompense. Yet the very forces which he himself has learnt to manipulate so brilliantly create new conflicts which he is incapable of understanding. Biffen shrinks from him when they meet; Milvain continues to the end to recognise his particular 'genius' yet despises him; and finally Whelpdale himself unconsciously states the traitor theme:

'Why in the name of sense and justice have I been suffered to attain this blessedness? Think of the days when I all but starved in my Albany Street garret, scarcely better off than poor, dear old Biffen! Why should I have come to this, and Biffen have poisoned himself in despair? He was a thousand times a better and cleverer fellow than I. And poor old Reardon, dead in misery! Could I for a moment compare with him?'

Milvain, as always, is ready to provide Whelpdale with the justification he seeks: 'You have exercised ingenuity and perseverance; you have your reward.'[1]

[1] Milvain is probably 'quoting' again: 'When therefore thou doest alms, sound not a trumpet before thee, as the hypocrites do in the synagogues and in the streets, that they may have glory of men. Verily I say unto you, They have received their reward.' Matthew, chap. 6, v. 2.

2. Artists

I

In Chapter III Milvain, returning from his country walk with Marian, stops to gaze at a horse: 'a poor worn-out beast, all skin and bone, which had presumably been sent here in the hope that a little more labour might still be exacted from it if it were suffered to repose for a few weeks. There were sores upon its back and legs; it stood in a fixed attitude of despondency, just flicking away troublesome flies with its grizzled tail.' The horse represents Reardon who although he does not actually appear until the fourth chapter has been a frequent subject of conversation in the preceding three. Like the horse Reardon wears himself out in ceaseless and thankless work, and his separation from Amy is to be finally brought about because of her plan for him to spend a brief, solitary holiday, from which he is to return freshened for further toil until death.

Reardon typifies the most common, and in many ways the most disturbing, kind of New Grub Street victim. According to Milvain's categories he is neither genius nor practical man. Nor is he a theorist like Biffen. Perhaps the most significant description of his work is given by Old John Yule:

> 'Just for curiosity I had a look at one of his books; it was called "The Optimist". Of all the morbid trash I ever saw, that beat everything. I thought of writing him a letter, advising a couple of anti-bilious pills before bedtime for a few weeks.'

This is intended as a common late Victorian, philistine, critical judgement and means much the same as Milvain's remark that Reardon's work is 'glaringly distinct from the ordinary circulating novel'. Biffen, as usual, is more precise when he describes his friend as 'a psychological realist in the sphere of culture'. If Reardon is no genius he clearly possesses an unusual talent which he attempts to bring to fruition by conscientious workmanship. It is his tragedy that he must try to make a living from literature in an age which has adopted public applause as the only possible form of patronage. In Chapter IV he makes this point himself:

'What an insane thing it is to make literature one's only means of support! When the most trivial accident may at any time prove fatal to one's power of work for weeks or months. No, that is the unpardonable sin! To make a trade of an art! I am rightly served for attempting such a brutal folly.'

He goes on to make a further important point:

'I am no uncompromising artistic pedant; I am quite willing to try and do the kind of work that will sell; under the circumstances it would be a kind of insanity if I refused. But power doesn't answer to the will.'

He accepts totally the view that if a book is popular then it must by definition be of poor quality, and likewise that a book which has considerable artistic value can never be a commercial success. When Amy argues that 'good work succeeds—now and then', he answers, 'I speak of the common kind of success, which is never due to literary merit.' Because he has a wife and child to support he cannot fight against the market; he must try to make concessions, and that means artistic suicide.

By nature he is a scholar who turns to fiction writing only after he fails to get his 'essays on literary subjects' published. In Chapter V where his early career is outlined it is shown that he was inspired to write novels by a glimpse of the luxurious home of a well-known author. At that moment he believed that literary or artistic success would bring financial and social rewards, and his marriage to Amy is his first step on the road to wealth and fame: 'He had always regarded the winning of a beautiful and intellectual wife as the crown of a successful literary career, but he had not dared to hope that such a triumph would be his.' It is, in fact, the only successful achievement of his career, just as it is also the ultimate cause of his destruction. He has been married just over a year when the novel opens and from this moment on the reputation he can already claim and his hopes for the future steadily decline.

In certain respects then, Reardon is not unlike Milvain. Where he differs is in his refusal to adjust his own literary standards according to the dictates of the market. He wants public acclamation but it must be on his own terms. It is an impossible demand and his dilemma is expressed in the traditional vocabulary of romantic agony: 'Often he fell into a fit of absence, and gazed at vacancy with wide, miserable eyes'; 'feverish determination to work'; 'racking his fagged brain'; 'torments of nightmare'; 'at times he was on the border-land of imbecility; his mind looked into a cloudy chaos, a shapeless whirl of nothings'. Such moments bring about a breakdown of the one quality which to his mind matters above all others—a good prose style:

> He would write a sentence beginning thus: 'She took a book with a look of——;' or thus: 'A revision of this decision would have made him an object of derision.' Or, if the period were otherwise inoffensive, it ran in a rhythmic gallop which was torment to the ear.

For such a person even the willingness to adapt his idealism to suit the market is useless. *Margaret Home*, his skimped three-volume novel, is acknowledged by everyone to be of poor quality; and his attempt at a one volume 'sensational' tale, written on Milvain's advice, is rejected by the publisher. Worse still, by writing novels which are inferior to his earlier work he knows full well that he will lose the small group of sympathetic readers he has acquired. His ideal society is that of *old* Grub Street where aristocratic patronage would, so he reasons, have given him the necessary security to publish only what he was not ashamed to acknowledge. In *new* Grub Street there is only one criterion by which literature is judged: 'The world has no pity on a man who can't do or produce something it thinks worth money. You may be a divine poet, and if some good fellow doesn't take pity on you you will starve by the roadside. Society is as blind and brutal as fate.' There is a further reason why Reardon looks back to *old* Grub Street as to a golden age. It was a time when the essayist, educated in the classics, was highly valued, and this is the part that Reardon could fill to perfection. He writes novels because this is the only type of literature which sells; it is the literary form to which everyone in *New Grub Street* turns at one time or another. Reardon himself makes the obvious comparison: 'A man who can't journalise, yet must earn his bread by literature, nowadays inevitably turns to fiction, as the Elizabethan men turned to the drama.' One of the most important reasons for Reardon's failure is that he really has no aptitude for or indeed love of fiction. Amy fully realises that novel writing is the only way to attain literary fame and that if Reardon was financially independent 'he would lapse into a life of scholarly self-indulgence, such as he had often told her was his ideal'. Money spent in this way, she reasons, would be money wasted. Even when Reardon does write essays there is little chance of selling them, for *Milvain* is the typical late Victorian essayist. He is the man of his day, and is thus fitted to note that Reardon 'sells a manuscript as if he lived in Sam Johnson's Grub Street'.

Remembering that his best novels were written in his free time while working as a hospital clerk, Reardon comes to believe that part-time writing is the modern equivalent of aristocratic patronage, and it is his determination to return to this system that brings his unhappy marriage to the breaking point:

'Coleridge wouldn't so easily meet with his Gillman nowadays. Well, I am not a Coleridge, and I don't ask to be lodged under any man's roof; but if I could earn money enough to leave me good long evenings unspoilt by fear of the workhouse—'

It is because of what Amy sneeringly calls his 'morbid conscientiousness' that he refuses to allow Milvain to help him with introductions and publicity. As much as he desires public recognition and entry into society life his pride will not allow him to attain these ends while his work is of an inferior quality. His tirades against the market are not symptomatic of an intellectual attitude but grow out of his disillusionment with his own ability. In Chapter XII when Amy urges him to model himself on Milvain, he answers: 'You lament that I can't write in that attractive way. Well, I lament it myself—for your sake. I wish I had Milvain's peculiar talent, so that I could get reputation and money. But I haven't, and there's an end of it.' The words 'for your sake' are only a way of getting back at Amy, for Reardon really does wish he was practical. The chapter heading of his death scene, *Reardon becomes Practical*, is ambiguous. He becomes practical at last by swallowing his pride and accepting Amy together with her new-found wealth; but it also indicates that his personality is such that death alone can stop his self-inflicted torture.

c

The destruction of Reardon is finally brought about not so much by his character, which is totally unfitted for the new style literary life, but by his marriage to Amy who is the mouthpiece of Milvain's theories. She is a traitor in much the same way as Whelpdale, and the various stages of her moral corruption are organised so as to emphasise this point. Reardon bitterly reminds her that during the early days of their marriage she was proud of him 'because my work wasn't altogether common, and because I had never written a line that was meant to attract the vulgar'. Her intellectual snobbery is merely a form of social distinction and she soon drops entirely her concern with literature as such and develops a new interest:

> She talked of questions such as international copyright, was anxious to get an insight into the practical conduct of journals and magazines, liked to know who 'read' for the publishing-houses. To an impartial observer it might have appeared that her intellect was growing more active and mature.

When she learns that her particular brand of intellectual snobbery can only be sustained by living perpetually on the edge of financial disaster, her whole attitude begins to change. Milvain, whom she had earlier treated with condescension—the natural feeling for the wife of an artist looking at a tradesman—now becomes to her the archetype of the literary man. His ideas she takes over wholesale, adding to them her own particular brand of venom: 'If I had to choose between a glorious reputation with poverty and a contemptible popularity with wealth, I should choose the latter.' It is the very choice which Reardon is incapable of making. His return to being a part-time author is for him the 'practical' way, while she is unable to recognise this use of the word. It is socially acceptable, she argues, for a literary man to have been poor, indeed it is expected of him, but to acknowledge that one can no longer make a full time living from literature is to confess to 'intellectual' decline. This point is further stressed in Chapter XXVI when Amy, now separated from Reardon, says to Mrs. Carter: 'My life is being wasted. I ought to have a place in the society of clever people. I was never meant to live quietly in the background.' Like Milvain she calls herself an intellectual because she recognises the practical way through life. Gissing underlines this point by referring to her 'noticeable maturing of intellect', since she has been living alone, which manifests itself in a passion for anything that savours 'of newness and boldness in philosophic thought.' At the same moment Reardon is declaring to Biffen that he can at last see that Amy was not a 'fit intellectual companion' for him. Amy's eventual marriage to Milvain is inevitable. From scorning him as the journeyman friend of her superior husband, she has progressed sufficiently to become his pupil, helped to destroy her husband, and on the way has become an 'intellectual' herself—she is his natural partner. It is the ironic theme of every success story in *New Grub Street* that intellectual pretension always accompanies moral corruption, and that to fall into poverty is to suffer both moral and intellectual degradation. Every character, except Biffen, would agree with Reardon on this subject:

'I have no sympathy with the stoical point of view; between wealth and poverty is just the difference between the whole man and the maimed. If my lower limbs are paralysed I may still be able to think, but then there is such a thing in life as walking. As a poor devil I may live nobly; but one happens to be made with faculties of enjoyment, and those have to fall into atrophy. To be sure, most rich people don't understand their happiness; if they did, they would move and talk like gods—which indeed they are.'

Reardon's decline, after his wife has left him, is far from convincing. From the beginning there has been a rather incongruous element of the romantic artist stereotype about him which has tended to weaken his representative role in the novel—that of the conscientious craftsman out of tune with the society in which he lives. In the early parts of the novel there are several aspects of this incongruity. One is the romantic terminology used to describe his struggle to write. Another is the way that his social failure induces in him extravagant bouts of self-pity. In Chapter IV, for instance, the self-pitying tone is apparent not merely in his own bursts of self-analysis, but in the detail which Gissing builds up around him: 'In the flat immediately beneath resided a successful musician, whose carriage and pair came at a regular hour each afternoon to take him and his wife for a most respectable drive.' Or, as he looks out of his window on to the backs of the houses opposite: 'in one room a man was discoverable dressing

for dinner, he had not thought it worthwhile to lower the blind; in
another, some people were playing billiards'. Or a more crude example
in Chapter XVII when the insensitive Mr. Carter chats amiably to
the impoverished Reardon about holidays in Scotland and Norway.
Many similar instances could be listed. They are intended to emphasis
the gap that exists between, on the one hand, Reardon's personality
and the life he is forced to lead; and on the other, Reardon's extreme
sensitivity and the increasing coarseness of society as a whole. They
lead up to the moment in Chapter XXVII when Reardon makes his
explicit statement on the finest end to which man can direct his life—
the contemplation of beautiful things:

> 'I am only maintaining that it is the best, and infinitely preferable to
> sexual emotion. It leaves, no doubt, no bitterness of any kind.
> Poverty can't rob me of those memories. I have lived in an ideal
> world that was not deceitful, a world which seems to me, when I
> recall it, beyond the human sphere, bathed in diviner light.'

But is is difficult to understand what good such moments have done
him. They exist solely in the mind; embalmed, as it were, in a vacuum.
They have certainly not helped calm his envy or jealousy. Indeed
the memories of his visit to Greece are used to reinforce his self-
pity.

The most disconcerting aspect of the characterisation of Reardon
is the extremely crude symbolism that is used to heighten his outcast
state. Left alone he decides to sell his furniture before moving to a new
lodging: 'These stripped rooms were symbolical of his life; losing
money, he had lost everything.' From this moment he is slowly
stripped of everything *save* his now regular earnings. He haunts out of
the way places, and in the streets he mutters snatches of poetry out
loud so that onlookers take him for a lunatic. The dual life which as
we have seen is his equivalent of patronage becomes merely a pose:

> He kept one suit of clothes for his hours of attendance at the
> hospital; it was still decent, and with much care would remain so
> for a long time. That which he wore at home and in his street
> wanderings declared poverty at every point; it had been discarded
> before he left the old abode. In his present state of mind he cared
> nothing how disreputable he looked to passers-by. These seedy

habiliments were the token of his degradation, and at times he regarded them (happening to see himself in a shop mirror) with pleasureable contempt.

While working at the hospital he asks a girl patient her occupation. She answers, 'I'm unfortunate, sir', and Reardon can barely resist the temptation to leap to his feet and shake her by the hand. Although he is now comparatively wealthy, free of ties, and has plenty of spare time, he comes to realise that Reardon the author is already dead, and Reardon the man wallows in the chance to suffer: 'An extraordinary arrogance now and then possessed him; he stood amid his poor surroundings with the sensations of an outraged exile, and laughed aloud in furious contempt of all who censured or pitied him.' In the two long sections in which Gissing speaks directly to the reader (the beginnings of Chapters XXV and XXI) it is made plain that Reardon's character *is* weak, that he does seek refuge in 'the passion of self-pity', but such confessions merely emphasise the flaw in this part of the book. It is a failure to convince that reaches its lowest point when first Reardon and then Biffen quote, at the moment of death, Prospero's lines from *The Tempest:* 'We are such stuff as dreams are made on, and our——'

Too often, in the characterisation of Reardon, it is obvious that Gissing is talking of himself and of his own position in New Grub Street. The bitterness and the loathing of society descends at times into an intolerable whine, which upsets the Milvain/Whelpdale/Reardon/Biffen balance. The reader soon becomes aware that certain character details given to Reardon, while they sometimes possess a relevance to the central themes of the book, are not integrated into the total pattern. One could instance such details as Reardon's pathological dread of hearing the workhouse bell; his pedantry over classical literature; his pleasure, when he moves to the slum, in 'contemplating the little collection of sterling books that alone remained to him from his library'; and his anti-democratic sentiments. The great strength of *New Grub Street* lies in the fact that it is a personal interpretation of the changing nature of literary culture in society; a personal vision which is artistically controlled and organised. It is because of this that excessive personal involvement with the feelings of one character constitutes a serious weakness in the novel.

II

Biffen is the only one of the literary figures who is not concerned with material success or failure. When Reardon asks him why he doesn't try to obtain a decent position he answers: 'No, no; it's all right. I keep myself alive, and I get on with my work.' Later, as his marriage crumbles around him, Reardon comes to see Biffen as the 'spoilt child of fortune', because if need be he 'could support life on three or four shillings a week, happy in the thought that no mortal had a claim upon him'. Reardon's fluctuating mood merely emphasises the gulf that separates the two friends. Biffen will make no compromise. He rejects the very society that has no interest in him or his work, and inhabits a world of loneliness and isolation which even Reardon only experiences at second hand. He accepts poverty and near starvation as his lot; living in out of the way places and earning enough money to keep alive by a kind of teaching 'quite unknown to the respectable tutorial world.' He even refuses to join Reardon in railing against the successful novelists, dismissing the subject in a manner curiously similar to that of Milvain:

'What does it matter? We are different types of intellectual workers. I think of them savagely now and then, but only when hunger gets a trifle too keen. Their work answers a demand; ours—or mine at all events—doesn't.'

Because he has accepted poverty as a natural condition of his life, he does not share Reardon's dread of tumbling down the social scale:

'I don't think I should be unhappy in the workhouse. I should have a certain satisfaction in the thought that I had forced society to support me. And then the absolute freedom from care! Why, it's very much the same as being a man of independent fortune.'

The echo of Milvain's speech in the first chapter is deliberate. For Biffen is the pure artist, and as such he is the hanged man, whom society does not support but gets rid of.

Biffen first appears in Chapter X and his unique qualities are immediately established. Although he joyfully enters into a pedantic discussion with Reardon on the scansion of Greek verse, he is also eager to advance his original theory of the novel. He is the only character who is consciously and fearlessly writing experimental fiction and he alone seems to possess an acquaintanceship with the work of some of the great nineteenth-century novelists. His theories of the 'ignobly decent' and the 'fateful power of trivial incidents', are to establish, when he can find a suitable subject, a form of realism which goes beyond that of either Dickens or Zola. Among other things Biffen wishes to handle the eternal subjects of farce in a serious, realistic manner:

> 'You know my stock instances of the kind of thing I mean. There was poor Allen, who lost the most valuable opportunity of his life because he hadn't a clean shirt to put on; and Williamson, who would probably have married that rich girl but for the grain of dust that got into his eye, and made him unable to say or do anything at the critical moment.'
> Reardon burst into a roar of laughter.
> 'There you are!' cried Biffen, with friendly annoyance. 'You take the conventional view. If you wrote of these things you would represent them as laughable.'
> 'They *are* laughable,' asserted the other, 'however serious to the persons concerned. The mere fact of grave issues in life depending on such paltry things is monstrously ludicrous. Life is a huge farce, and the advantage of possessing a sense of humour is that it enables one to defy fate with mocking laughter.'

But the laugh is on Reardon, for when, much later in the novel, he goes to visit Amy hoping for a reconciliation with her, the meeting is completely ruined by his shabby appearance. Amy is ashamed of her feelings but she acknowledges the power they have upon her actions: 'She had been doubtful till now, but all doubt was at an end. Had Reardon been practical man enough to procure by hook or by crook a decent suit of clothes for this interview, that ridiculous trifle might have made all the difference in what was to result.' It is a perfect example of the 'fateful power of trivial incidents', and Biffen, in his role of realistic observer, is completely vindicated. While Reardon seems to argue that the 'art of fiction' is something which is stable and fixed (an attitude which is symptomatic of his own difficulties, both literary and personal), Biffen wants to reject all conventions and to break new ground regardless of the opinions of public or friends. It is significant that he first met Reardon because 'an abusive review had interested him in Reardon's novels'; it is further significant that Reardon openly laughs at Biffen's theories, taking, as the artist points out, 'the conventional view'. Yet in spite of this Reardon does recognise the true worth of Biffen's efforts—the courage, the honesty, and the refusal to place himself under any obligation which would interfere with his creative work. Gissing returns to this point in Chapter XXXI when he addresses to the reader a defence of such passive, unpractical people:

> He worked very slowly. The book would make perhaps two volumes of ordinary novel size, but he had laboured over it for many months, patiently, affectionately, scrupulously. Each sentence was as good as he could make it, harmonious to the ear, with words of precious meaning skilfully set. Before sitting down to a chapter he planned it minutely in his mind; then he wrote a rough draft of it; then he elaborated the thing phrase by phrase. He had no thought of whether such toil would be recompensed in coin of the realm; nay, it was his conviction that, if with difficulty published, it could scarcely bring him money. The work must be significant, that was all he cared for. And he had no society of admiring friends to encourage him. Reardon understood the merit of the workmanship, but frankly owned that the book was repulsive to him. To the public it would be worse than repulsive—tedious, utterly uninteresting. No matter; it drew to its end.

It is the most overt statement on the position of the artist which is made in *New Grub Street*. The conscientious craftsmanship that Reardon longs to develop and which Milvain mocks can be attained only by completely withdrawing from all social and personal relationships; by accepting the possibility of starvation, and by expecting no reward other than inner satisfaction.

Through Biffen the reader also catches a rare glimpse of a Murger type of bohemianism. Scenes such as Biffen refusing to remove his overcoat because he has pawned his only jacket; or his eating bread and dripping with a knife and fork in order to make his meal seem more substantial, represent moments when Gissing is losing his grip and seems in danger of toppling over into an idealisation of artistic poverty. But although moments such as these tend to weaken the total presentation of Biffen, they by no means predominate. In contrast Chapter XXVII in which Biffen takes Reardon to meet the alcoholic Sykes, opens up an area of literary life involving poverty and degradation of a kind known to Biffen but of which Reardon is completely ignorant. The account of Sykes's literary career is a typical device which Gissing employs to expand the significance of his central conflicts to a wider society. In the past Sykes has displayed literary talents on a scale which even Milvain might envy: 'I could throw off my supplemental novelette of fifteen thousand words without turning a hair, and immediately after it fall to, fresh as a daisy, on the "Illustrated History of the United States", which I was then doing for Edward Coghlan.' In an attempt to make a 'reputation' he begins to write three-volume novels, fails at this and returns to his old trade, only to find that the artistic skill he so carefully developed has destroyed the journalistic facility he once possessed. Now an alcoholic he is obliged to write in some shabby public reading-rooms, compiling his autobiography *Through the Wilds of Literary London* for the *Shropshire Weekly Herald*.

Chapter XXXI in which Biffen nearly dies saving the completed manuscript of *Mr. Bailey, Grocer* from a fire, is meant to be symbolic of the way the artist sacrifices his life for his work, but it is not wholly successful. Once again, however, this rather bohemianised adventure does, with the aid of some weak satire, afford a glimpse of a society which cares for neither Biffen nor his novel. The moral is neatly put when Biffen wonders whether to tell a publisher that he has risked his life saving the manuscript in the hope that the work might be accepted out of sympathy. This is, of course, just the kind of thing that could inspire a New Grub Street publisher to accept the novel, but for reasons totally unlike those envisaged by Biffen. It recalls Milvain's earlier remark that 'If a man can't hit upon any other way of attracting attention, let him dance on his head in the middle of the street; after that he may hope to get consideration for his volume of poems.' Had Milvain been at hand to offer advice he would have determined to squeeze the maximum publicity out of the fire incident. But Reardon and Biffen relieve the tension by grimly joking about the attitudes that various newspapers might have adopted should the artist have died in the fire. 'The *Saturday*,' Biffen says, 'would have had a column of sneering jocosity on the irrepressibly sanguine temperament of authors.' In a strange way the two friends feel that they have scored a victory over the press. In New Grub Street, however, the power of press is absolute and when *Mr. Bailey*, *Grocer* appears, the reviewers, even without any knowledge of the fire, have a field day.

> 'Let Mr. Biffen bear in mind,' said one of these sages, 'that a novelist's first duty is to tell a story.' 'Mr. Biffen,' wrote another, 'seems not to understand that a work of art must before everything else afford amusement.' 'A pretentious book of the *genre ennuyant*,' was the brief comment of a Society journal.

Biffen's greatest strength as a man and an artist lies in his inability to develop a cynical attitude to life. He is shown to be completely honest with himself and others; refusing to take the much needed money from pupils who he felt were not worth teaching, and keeping silent on the subject of Reardon's skimped novel. The years of constant deprivation lead him to develop a philosophy of quietism which disturbingly heightens his personal and social isolation. All forms of suffering are accepted because to struggle in such a world would only invite the infliction of further pain. Even the commercial failure of his novel is no cause for additional pessimism: 'It was no more than he anticipated. The work was done—the best he was capable of—and this satisfied him.' It is because his own view of life is the product of constant suffering that he urges Reardon to return to Amy and attempt to salvage what he can from the broken relationship to make a happy marriage. He has long since realised that Reardon does not possess the necessary acceptance of pain that makes a great writer and Biffen's advice to his friend is ironic in that the only person his common sense cannot apply to is himself:

> 'What are we—you and I? . . . We have no belief in immortality; we are convinced that this life is all; we know that human happiness is the origin and end of all moral considerations. What right have we to make ourselves and others miserable for the sake of an obstinate idealism? It is our duty to make the best of circumstances.'

It is the final irony in Biffen's career that his suicide is ultimately inspired by Amy Reardon who, although Biffen will never believe it, has long since become a spokesman for the commercial ethic.

Gissing makes it perfectly clear that of all the sufferings that beset the solitary literary man, that of sexual frustration is the most disruptive. Alfred Yule marries a shop girl because 'the time had come when he could not do without a wife'. Whelpdale makes himself a figure of ridicule because he proposes to every attractive girl he meets. Milvain's customary composure is shattered when he first meets Marian and his conversations about her show that he is well aware of the 'dangers' closer friendship might entail. Further, it is difficult not to draw the conclusion that the breakdown of Reardon's marriage is not merely social but sexual as well. Reardon's early years had been passed in 'monkish solitude'; and the coldness he shows towards his child, his repeated assertion that he 'ought to have looked about for some simple, kind-hearted work girl', and the way that Amy shrinks from his touch, are all details which show that Reardon, although he is married, suffers the same kind of frustration as his single friends. Biffen rejects all thought of obtaining a beautiful woman to share his poverty stricken life. It is a yet further deprivation he consciously suffers and the result is his absolute idealisation of Amy, who is the only beautiful woman he knows who has gone to live with a struggling writer. So obsessed is he with the thought that one day similar good fortune might fall to him that he even listens with interest to the narration of Whelpdale's farcical romantic adventures. He knows too much of life to follow Yule's example and marry a working-girl, and when Reardon countenances such a view it is Biffen who points out the common-sense objections. There are hints now and later that Biffen has had an unhappy love affair in the past, but like all biographical details about him these remain obscure. With the death of Reardon and the publication of *Mr. Bailey, Grocer*, Biffen once again comes into contact with Amy. Her extravagant praise of his novel followed by his social inability to enter the world she inhabits places a new strain on him:

> The poor fellow was so lonely. Yes, but his loneliness only became intolerable when a beautiful woman had smiled upon him, and so forced him to dream perpetually of that supreme joy which to him was forbidden.

44 NEW GRUB STREET

To commit suicide he travels out to Putney Hill, dying, as he lived, an outcast. Thinking of Amy he links her in his mind with those moments of Ideal Art which he and Reardon had viewed as things unique, in that their contemplation caused only joy. Thus in the end Biffen too is fooled and defeated by commercialism. It is a force so insidious that no one can really escape.

3. Men of Letters

Like Reardon, Alfred Yule is a victim of both his own personality and the market. Like Whelpdale, he is a failed novelist who has turned his attention to other fields. Like Milvain, he is involved in a world of editors, reviewers, critics and literary gossip. Like Biffen and Reardon, he possesses an intellect which has no market value. Of all the major figures in *New Grub Street* he is the only one whose career is behind him. He is a failure who is still hoping for his one last chance to blaze into literary glory; a chance which should it come to him, would be used not to create but to destroy. He exists in the novel as a permanent warning of the destructive element that exists in all of the younger ambitious writers.

The world of literary gossip, self-seeking and rivalry is presented by Milvain as a kind of game, a game with a deadly seriousness of purpose underneath, but none the less something to laugh and joke about. The example of Alfred Yule shows that same world as sour and squalid. Once a promising young editor himself who became involved in a literary duel which could do him nothing but harm, he now earns most of his money by writing anonymous articles, or deputing Marian to write them, on obscure literary themes. His formidable intellect and pedantic style of writing are useless weapons with which to wage the retributive battle he dreams of. Around him he gathers his group of shabby and intellectually inferior friends, who wait upon his reinstatement in an editor's chair, like courtiers surrounding an exiled king. Together they plot the return to power, a movement which culminates in Chapter XXIII when they fawn upon Marian, whom they have hitherto treated as a drudge, in an attempt to get her to 'invest' her small legacy in a new magazine. It is to be a purely 'literary' venture, and is to fill a gap in the market:

> 'The thing would pay its way almost from the first. It would take a place between the literary weeklies and the quarterlies. The former are too academic, the latter too massive, for multitudes of people who yet have strong literary tastes. Foreign publications

should be liberally dealt with. But, as Hinks says, no meddling with the books that are no books—*biblia abiblia;* nothing about essays on bimetallism and treatises for or against vaccination'.

Even here, in the freedom of a friend's study, he laughed his Reading-room laugh, folding both hands upon his expansive waistcoat.

'Fiction? I presume a serial of the better kind might be admitted?' said Yule.

'That would be advisable, no doubt. But strictly of the better kind.'

'Oh, strictly of the better kind,' chimed in Mr. Hinks.

But in spite of Alfred Yule's sweetness of tone in this scene, his heart is set on employing the new magazine to wreak vengeance on his enemies. Once he would have thought differently but now he views literature as a personal weapon to strike back at those who caused his editorial failure. The book he publishes called *English Prose in the Nineteenth Century* serves to illustrate the theme that 'journalism is the destruction of prose style', and temporarily stirs up the literary world to scornful abuse: 'For the moment people talked more of Alfred Yule than they had done since his memorable conflict with Clement Fadge.' Here is one kind of fame and, at this stage of his life, the kind that Alfred Yule most desires.

In the presentation of Alfred Yule Gissing concentrates on his relationships with his wife and daughter in order to emphasise the corrupting effect that literary ambition can have upon personal life. When, in Chapter XXI, Yule has his long argument with the vulgar Mrs. Goby, she strikes exactly the right note when she rebukes him with, 'though I dare say a gentleman as has so many books about him can correct me if I've made a mistake'. For in spite of his book-learning and the great fund of erudite knowledge upon which he draws for his essay subjects, Yule has no understanding of either his own character or the feelings of other people. In both his career and his marriage he has been a failure, and the only joy he can now find is in the exercise of his tedious pedantry. He is almost happy as he walks in the country with Milvain, lecturing the young tradesman on the neglected merits of Shadwell and chuckling over dry, professional jokes. In the family dinner scene (Chapter VII) his black mood turns

to one of joy as he contemplates a new book that has been presented
to him:

> His eyes glinted, his chin worked in pleasurable emotion. In a
> moment he handed the book to Marian, indicating the small type
> of a foot-note; it embodied an effusive eulogy—introduced *à
> propos* of some literary discussion—of 'Mr. Alfred Yule's critical
> acumen, scholarly research, lucid style,' and sundry other dis-
> tinguished merits.

This moment of happiness is only fleeting: for few books contain such
a pleasant surprise as this. With the meal over he gives Marian some
more work to do: 'When you have time I want you to read Ditchley's
new book, and jot down a selection of his worst sentences. I'll use
them for an article on contemporary style; it occurred to me this afternoon.' The bile is never far from the surface and his spite is vented on
friends, enemies and relatives alike. Even when he knows it to be
false he keeps alive the rumour that Milvain was the author of a viru-
lently critical review of his latest book; thus flattering his own
irrational prejudices and tormenting his daughter. Marian herself
gives the reason for his perverse behaviour: 'Literary quarrels have
made you incapable of judging honestly in things such as this.'

The cause of his early marriage has already been looked at but what
should be mentioned is the loathing with which he treats his wife. His
failure to rise in New Grub Street is because he does not possess the
necessary talents. Like Reardon, 'he was living in a past age; his literary
ideals were formed on the study of Boswell'—but his own guilty
knowledge of early sexual weakness, forces him to place the full
responsibility for his failure on his working-class wife. She must bear
the brunt of his violent temper and spiteful remarks, and must suffer
the terrible indignity of watching her daughter deliberately educated
to despise the mother's accent and lack of learning. Yule's domestic
tyranny is symbolic of the literary tyranny he wishes to exert. They
are both the product of frustrated intellect—a quality which in *New
Grub Street* is self-destructive unless it can be bolstered up with money
or influence.

The most terrible effects of Alfred Yule's character are seen at work
upon Marian. She is the person most associated with the British

Museum Reading-room where her own talents, which are shown to
be considerable, are slowly withered away by her subjugation to her
father's will. In Chapter VIII she gives way to the despair that her
family life has always encouraged. Surrounded by mountains of
books in the Reading-room, Marian realises with horror that the
continual grind of literary production of the kind she and her father
are involved in, is merely an avoidance of main issues, a retreat from
true literature:

> What unspeakable folly! To write—was not that the joy and the
> privilege of one who had an urgent message for the world? Her
> father, she knew well, had no such message; he had abandoned all
> thought of original production, and only wrote about writing. . . .
> And all these people about her, what aim had they save to make
> new books out of those already existing, that yet newer books
> might in turn be made out of theirs?

She watches an official walking round the upper gallery and imagines
him 'a black, lost soul, doomed to wander in an eternity of vain
research along endless shelves'. From this moment she has no faith in
literature, and her love for Milvain symbolises her changed attitude.
She has no illusions about his true character but at least he represents
one form of vitality. Throughout the novel she is associated with fog
imagery and it is Milvain who is to lead her into the light.[1] He in turn
is physically attracted to her and explains away this unwelcome
feeling by pronouncing her to be his intellectual equal. But like her
father Marian must learn that intellect is not enough: for if the values
by which Yule lives are rotten so are those advocated by Milvain.
In the depth of her despair she had thought: 'Oh, to go forth and
labour with one's hands, to do any poorest, commonest work of
which the world had truly need!' and this, indeed, is what she is
eventually forced to do. It does not however, represent freedom. As
a country librarian she is finally condemned to the very world she had
longed to opt out of.

The curious little scene in Chapter XXIX when Yule's blindness is
diagnosed by a down and out surgeon, is unsatisfactory. It clumsily

---

[1] In Chapter III a different image is used. Milvain, in Marian's eyes, is
the oak, which, as she tells him, is the only tree she can recognise.

brings together two victims of fate and this slightly undermines the importance of Yule's character. For he is the 'black, lost soul' wandering along endless shelves of books, and although his blindness is an obvious symbol of his wasted literary life, it is also symbolic of his inability to understand life as opposed to literature. The man of letters is an anachronism in New Grub Street and Gissing shows that to fight against this fact is to invite disaster. The world of the periodicals now belongs to Milvain. The reading public has no time for the 'conscientious' work of Alfred Yule. It is fitting that his death should be announced at Milvain's victory party, and that the news should be presented as a piece of gossip.

4. *Readers*

When Reardon says of his failed sensational novel: 'The thing is too empty to please the better kind of readers, yet not vulgar enough to please the worse', he reveals an attitude of mind which is shared, in different ways, by every literary figure in *New Grub Street*. It is assumed throughout the novel that the 'vulgar' constitute the majority and that the actual number of 'the better kind of readers' is very small indeed. In general terms each writer is fully aware of the type of reader his work will attract. Whelpdale writes for the 'quarter-educated'; Milvain for the intellectually pretentious; Reardon for a 'small section of refined readers'; Yule for whoever reads the more solid periodicals; and Biffen for himself. But who exactly are these readers? Are they divided by class or by education? Are the vulgar necessarily the lower classes? And how far are the answers to these questions influenced by Gissing's own prejudices and obsessions?

There are three main groups of readers. First, the literary figures themselves. Second, the relatives and friends of the literary figures; and third, the minor, lower or working-class characters. Of the first group Reardon, Yule and Biffen as intellectuals all possess a great love of literature, but only Biffen seems to have any interest in or feeling for contemporary writing. Whelpdale is never seriously mentioned in connection with reading. Milvain employs the literature of the past as a gigantic source for relevant quotations, and his knowledge of contemporary literature to write reviews which are used to make friends rather than pass critical judgement. This last point is especially important as everyone recognises the great influence that the reviews have on how the libraries spend their money, what the reading public turns to, and whether or not the author succeeds or fails. Furthermore Milvain's influential acquaintances are always represented as having no feeling for literature as anything but a salable commodity. Thus the tradesmen can hardly be classified as readers—so far as they are concerned a total break with literary tradition is to their advantage. The artists and the men of letters, on the other hand, are conscious of their role in a total cultural heritage, but their interests and the

expression of those interests are so pedantic that the tradition to which
they look back can hardly be said to be living. Biffen avoids both
extremes and he alone has no readers.

Of the second group, Marian and Dora are shown to possess sound
critical abilities, although Marian grows to hate all literature, and
Dora's marriage to Whelpdale is intended to show that if she is
sensible she is also shallow. Maud, however, signifies a different type
altogether. In Chapter XXXIV we learn that Maud's rise from being
the authoress of 'Sunday school prizes' to the wife of a wealthy man,
is to her material advantage but detrimental to literature:

> Maud was established in the midst of luxuries, and talked with
> laughing scorn of the days when she inhabited Grub Street;
> her literary tastes were henceforth to serve as merely a note of
> distinction, an added grace which made evident her superiority to
> the well-attired and smooth-tongued people among whom she was
> content to shine. On the one hand, she had contact with the world
> of fashionable literature, on the other with that of fashionable
> ignorance.

The poles within which Maud moves are both equally despised by
Gissing—'fashionable literature' is as bad as 'fashionable ignorance'.
It is, of course, between these two extremes that Reardon had hoped
to drive a wedge. Mr. and Mrs. Carter, in their friendship with the
Reardons, take Maud's attitude one step further. Mr. Carter is an
amiable philistine who frankly bows before his clerk's superior intellect
and accepts Reardon's eccentric behaviour as being appropriate
to a writer. But his wife, equally amiable and philistine, wallows in
the snobbery that an unsuccessful, *good* author can generate. She treats
Reardon with awe, even tiptoeing up to look at the blank sheets
of paper on his desk when he is out; to her it is a source of considerable pride that she is friendly with an author who cannot make a
living from writing. 'You don't expect ordinary novel-readers to
know about Mr. Reardon' she says to Amy.

Amy's mother, Mrs. Edmund Yule, is the complete Gissing snob:
'Her circle was not large, but in that circle she must be regarded with
the respect due to a woman of refined tastes and personal distinction.'
She is an 'intellectual' of a similar stamp to her daughter and Milvain,

giving her permission for the marriage on Amy's assurance that Reardon would soon 'have a reputation far other than that of the average successful storyteller'. As the truth dawns on her that any reputation that Reardon is likely to gain will not be convertible into hard cash, she immerses herself in the whole elaborate mystique of the eccentric artist. His strange habits, his talking in his sleep, his inability to make a living, his 'out-of-the-way interests'—anything but his actual books or conscientious craftsmanship is used to defend her own maternal error. Finally she even convinces herself that he had actually become a 'successful' author and had deliberately abandoned his career. Madness is the only plausible explanation. Her son, John Yule, exhibits a degree of ignorance to which even his mother does not sink:

'Confound the fellow! Why the deuce doesn't he go on with his novel writing? There's plenty of money to be made out of novels.'
'But he can't write, Jack. He has lost his talent.'
'That's all bosh, Amy. If a fellow has once got into the swing of it he can keep it up if he likes. He might write his two novels a year easily enough, just like twenty other men and women. Look here, I could do it myself if I weren't too lazy. And that's what's the matter with Reardon. He doesn't care to work.'

The upper middle-class world, then, even when it comes in personal contact with the artist, has no understanding of his unique role in society. While Reardon is walking the streets racking his brain for a plot, Mrs. Carter is saying to Amy: 'How delightful it must be to sit down and write about people one has invented! Ever since I have known you and Mr. Reardon I have been tempted to try if I couldn't write a story.' This ever increasing gulf that separates the author from the reader is just one part of the fragmentation of the social consciousness, along with Amy's obsession with the personal details of the private lives of celebrities, Whelpdale's snippets of information, and the publicity antics fostered by the publishers. The corrupting effect of this process of cultural avoidance is clearly shown when Amy, freed from the influence of her husband, begins to develop her intellect: 'She read a good deal of that kind of literature which may be defined as specialism popularised; writing which addresses itself to educated, but not strictly studious, persons, and which forms the reservoir of

conversation for society above the sphere of turf and west-endism. . . .
She was becoming a typical woman of the new time, the woman who
has developed concurrently with journalistic enterprise.' Women it
seems are particularly susceptible to these kinds of pressure. They
have more spare time to devote to reading than the men; they domi-
nate social life; and the Married Woman's Property Act (1882) has
made them more independent of their husbands. Amy proclaims the
Act 'the only one worth anything that I ever heard of'. Gissing himself would clearly not agree with this sentiment. His own view is
given in Chapter III when he outlines the home background of
Milvain's sisters:

> Their life had a tone of melancholy, the painful reserve which
> characterises a certain clearly defined class in the present day. Had
> they been born twenty years earlier, the children of that veterinary
> surgeon would have grown up to a very different, and in all prob-
> ability a much happier existence, for their education would have
> been limited to the strictly needful, and—certainly in the case of
> the girls—nothing would have encouraged them to look beyond
> the simple life possible to a poor man's offspring.

Reardon too believes this. When he finds he can no longer order Amy
to do what he wishes he says: 'I begin to see how much right there is
on the side of those people who would keep women in subjection.
You have been allowed to act with independence, and the result is
that you have ruined my life and debased your own.' The word
'debased' is particularly important, for Amy has changed sides. She
has ceased to defend the artist and has become a typical middle-class
reader; she is now part of a group which has lost all interest in literature while developing a voracious appetite for 'specialism popularised'.
Because he has been educated for better things the middle-class reader
is, at heart, aware of his betrayal, and as compensation for his feelings
of guilt he constructs a mythical artist before whose image he can pay
obeisance.

The group of working-class characters reveal even more clearly
Gissing's own attitudes. The loud-mouthed Mrs. Goby, Mr. Baker
the examination candidate who Biffen teaches, the furniture dealer
who buys Reardon's broken home, and the characters who appear

during the fire scene in Chapter XXXI are all despised by Gissing. They are totally insensitive and thus inferior to the people with whom they come in contact. Their coarseness is illustrated by the use of primitive phonetic spelling to represent their low speech: 'I am Mrs. Goby, of the 'Olloway Road, wife of Mr. C. O. Goby, 'aberdasher'. Mr. Baker, in personality the most attractive of the working-class characters, is allowed to speak almost normally save for pronouncing 'composition' as 'compersition'—a solitary distinction which is merely snobbery on the part of the author. Further, Mr. Baker's struggle to improve his education is used to make a cheap comparison with Reardon's creative agony:

> 'I can make headway with the other things, sir . . . There's handwriting, there's orthography, there's arithmetic; I'm not afraid of one of 'em, as Mr. Biffen'll tell you, sir. But when it comes to compersition, that brings out the sweat on my forehead, I do assure you.'
> 'You're not the only man in that case, Mr. Baker,' replied Reardon.
> 'It's thought a tough job in general, is it, sir?'
> 'It is indeed.'

There are several such moments as this. When Reardon is dying in Brighton, Amy explains to the nurse that her husband undermined his strength by writing when he needed a rest. 'I always thought it must be hard work writing books,' the nurse answers. Or again, after Biffen has rescued his manuscript from the fire he sits bemoaning the loss of his books. The man he is talking to sympathises with him thinking that Biffen means his *account* books. This is the kind of irony that rebounds upon Gissing, for who exactly is being got at? Are Milvain and Whelpdale responsible for this type of ignorance? Surely not; for if that were the case then Mr. Baker's examination attempt would be a praiseworthy move to counterbalance the evil. But he is only mocked for his efforts.

Whenever lower-class characters appear Gissing cannot resist the temptation to point out their sluggish ignorance. They are not re-garded as individuals, no matter what part they play in the novel, but are always discussed in general class terms. Gissing's rather ambiguous treatment of Mrs. Alfred Yule is a good example of this:

Mrs. Yule's speech was seldom ungrammatical, and her intonation
was not flagrantly vulgar, but the accent of the London poor, which
brands as with hereditary baseness, still clung to her words, render-
ing futile such propriety of phrase as she owed to years of association
with educated people.

She is shown to be an excellent mother, to have virtually superhuman
patience, and to be the innocent victim of Alfred Yule's verbal
brutality. Yet in spite of this Gissing still thinks it sufficiently important to stress that her accent brands as with hereditary baseness. Nor
is it allowed to rest at that. He goes on: 'The London work-girl is
rarely capable of raising herself, or being raised, to a place in life
above that to which she was born; she cannot learn how to stand and
sit and move like a woman bred to refinement, any more than she can
fashion her tongue to graceful speech.' But Gissing's own values here
seem to be confused. The women in *New Grub Street* who have been
'bred to refinement' may be able to sit and stand gracefully but in all
other respects they are shown, with the exception of Marian Yule, to
be petty-minded, materialistic and intellectually shallow. This is one
of those curious moments, common in his other novels but rare in
this one, when Gissing seems willing to sacrifice completely his moral
standpoint in exchange for a little surface charm.

When he introduces the furniture dealer Gissing notes that he 'was
a rough and rather dirty fellow, with the distrustful glance which
distinguishes his class'. And even the Reardons' maidservant who appears fleetingly is described as being 'recently emancipated from the
Board school'. Education is no good because the working classes only
use it to get jobs or to run businesses, and not to read Greek tragedies
or even Reardon's novels. In between they no doubt read *Chit-Chat*,
but that cannot be a corrupting force because education is shown to be
useless in their case. And besides the scene on the island of Sark shows
that it is the middle classes who are seduced away from more solid
reading by *Chit-Chat*.

What then is to happen to the working classes? Gissing himself
saw no hope for them whatsoever, but there is an alternative solution
advanced in *New Grub Street*. In Chapter II Old John Yule puts
forward his plan. It is his money that is eventually to determine the
fate of many of the literary figures, and, significantly, his wealth has

come from the manufacture of paper. It is a joke on this subject that leads him into his tirade: 'I wish ... that you were both condemned to write on such paper as I chiefly made; it was a special kind of whitey-brown, used by shopkeepers.' The use to which his listeners customarily put paper is scorned by him. He loathes literary men and what he considers is the debilitating effect of excessive reading:

'Your Board schools, your popular press, your spread of education! Machinery for ruining the country, that's what I call it.'

At times Gissing talks in a similar tone:

In these days of examinations, numbers of men in a poor position—clerks chiefly—conceive a hope that by 'passing' this, that, or the other formal test they may open for themselves a new career. Not a few such persons nourish preposterous ambitions; there are warehouse clerks privately preparing (without any means or prospect of them) for a call to the Bar, drapers' assistants who 'go in' for the preliminary examination of the College of Surgeons, and untaught men innumerable who desire to procure enough show of education to be eligible for a curacy.

Gissing's sarcastic employment of the terminology of examination candidates in this passage shows clearly where he stands in the matter. It is a rather hysterical case of railing against those who confuse the passing of examinations with educational development. Old John Yule does not really argue like this. His theories are not merely the result of bad temper or philistinism. He is quite ready to offer a positive, alternative system:

'Go about the Continent, and see the effect of military service on loutish peasants and the lowest classes of town population. Do you know why it isn't even more successful? Because the damnable education movement interferes. If Germany would shut up her schools and universities for the next quarter of a century and go ahead like blazes with military training there'd be a nation such as the world has never seen. After that, they might begin a little book-teaching again—say an hour and a half a day for everyone above nine years old. Do you suppose, Mr. Milvain, that society is going to be reformed by you people who write for money? Why, you are the very first class that will be swept from the face of the earth as soon as the reformation really begins!'

That Gissing himself does not sympathise with this view is clear from his satirical treatment of Old John Yule. This particular vision of 'civilisation' is intended to express the fear that Gissing felt at the growth of Prussian militarism. But is his own view so very different? Gissing presents his upper- and middle-class characters as being shallow and pretentious. He presents his lower-class characters as little better than animals (although the working-class girls are sexually attractive enough animals to serve as mistresses to the intellectuals), and he scorns the power of education to bring about any worthwhile changes in them. Old John Yule would go much of the way with this but argues further that the working classes should at least be turned into *healthy* animals. Gissing would not countenance *this*, but he can offer no satisfactory alternative.

In *New Grub Street* Gissing set out to analyse a whole society's response to literary culture. He found no genuine response at all and could see no hope for the future. The forces of commercialism, symbolised by the triumphant careers of Milvain and Whelpdale, sweep all before them: destroying the craftsman, ignoring the artist and blinding the man of letters. Standing silently in the background is the reading public—a vast, inert, helpless and hopeless mass. Totally unaware that a struggle is taking place the great majority of readers surrender their minds to the tradesmen, adopting the second rate as the norm and rejecting as worthless that which they are incapable of understanding. Every attempt to actively oppose, or establish a compromise with the forces of commercialism, is doomed to failure; for such an attempt can lead only to an undermining of one's own integrity, a foreshortening of one's own vision. All the artist can do is turn his back on society.

On 22nd September, 1885, in a letter to his brother, Gissing expressed his horror at William Morris's involvement with socialism. Gissing felt that Morris should stand aside from all questions of social reform and 'write poetry in the shade'. The artist, he argues, has no commitment save to himself and his work: 'Keep apart, keep apart, and preserve one's soul alive—that is the teaching for the day. It is ill to have been born in these times, but one can make a world within a world.' This sombre view might stand as a preface to *New Grub Street*. As society collapses around him the artist must play no part in attempting to stop the rot, but should retreat into his private world, alone and isolated. Only thus can art survive.

Gissing's vision is therefore one of bleak pessimism, but it is saved from total despair by a faith in the ability of a few men to nurture the stoical qualities necessary for survival in a hostile world. The relevance today of Gissing's study of a commercially divided culture scarcely needs pointing, for if the conclusions he reaches are disheartening, his analysis is shot through with brilliant insight and perception. *New Grub Street* remains a profoundly disturbing book.

Select Bibliography

Letters

Letters of George Gissing to Members of his family, collected and arranged by Algernon and Ellen Gissing, London (1927)

The Letters of George Gissing to Eduard Bertz, 1887–1903, edited by Arthur C. Young, London (1961)

Biographical and Critical Studies

Donnelly, Mabel Collins, *George Gissing: Grave Comedian*, Cambridge, Mass. (1954)

Korg, Jacob, *George Gissing, A Critical Biography*, London (1965)

Secombe, Thomas, Introduction to George Gissing, *The House of Cobwebs*, London (1906)

Swinnerton, Frank, *George Gissing, A Critical Study*, London (1912)

Articles

Francis, C. J., *Gissing and Schopenhauer*, Nineteenth-Century Fiction, XV 1960

Gross, John, Introduction to *New Grub Street*, Bodley Head, London (1967)

Howe, Irving, Introduction to *New Grub Street*, Riverside Editions, Boston (1962)

Korg, Jacob, *Division of Purpose in George Gissing*, PMLA, LXX 1955

Leavis, Q. D., *Gissing and the English Novel*, Scrutiny, VII 1938

Woolf, Virginia, Introduction to *Selections Autobiographical and Imaginative from the Works of George Gissing*, edited by A. C. Gissing, London (1929)

The articles by Francis, Howe and Korg, are included in *Collected Articles on George Gissing*, edited by Pierre Coustillas, London (1967)

Background

Altick, Richard D., *The English Common Reader*, Chicago (1957)
Leavis, Q. D., *Fiction and the Reading Public*, London (1932)
Williams, Raymond, *Culture and Society*, London (1958)
—— *The Long Revolution*, London (1961)

Index